COOL
GAME DAY
PARTIES

Beyond the Basics for Kids Who Cook

LISA
WAGNER

A Division of ABDO

ABDO
Publishing Company

Visit us at www.abdopublishing.com

Published by ABDO Publishing Company, P.O. Box 398166, Minneapolis, MN 55439. Copyright ©2014 by Abdo Consulting Group, Inc. International copyrights reserved in all countries. No part of this book may be reproduced in any form without written permission from the publisher. The Checkerboard Library™ is a trademark and logo of ABDO Publishing Company.

Printed in the United States of America, North Mankato, Minnesota
102013
012014

 PRINTED ON RECYCLED PAPER

Editor: Liz Salzmann
Content Developer: Nancy Tuminelly
Cover and Interior Design and Production: Colleen Dolphin, Mighty Media, Inc.
Food Production: Desirée Bussiere
Photo Credits: Colleen Dolphin, Shutterstock

Library of Congress Cataloging-in-Publication Data
Wagner, Lisa, 1958- author.
  Cool game day parties : beyond the basics for kids who cook / Lisa Wagner.
       pages cm. -- (Cool young chefs)
  Audience: Ages 8 to 12.
  Includes bibliographical references and index.
  ISBN 978-1-62403-088-8
  1. Snack foods--Juvenile literature. 2. Cooking, American--Juvenile literature. 3. Parties--Juvenile literature. I. Title.
  TX740.W2143 2014
  641.5'68--dc23
                          2013022529

TO ADULT HELPERS

Congratulations on being the proud parent of an up-and-coming chef! This series of books is designed for children who have already done some cooking—most likely with your guidance and encouragement. Now, with some of the basics out of the way, it's time to really get cooking!

The focus of this series is on parties and special events. The "Big Idea" is all about the creative side of cooking (mastering a basic method or recipe and then using substitutions to create original recipes). Listening to your young chef's ideas for new creations and sharing your own ideas and experiences can lead to exciting (and delicious) discoveries!

While the recipes are designed to let children cook independently as much as possible, you'll need to set some ground rules for using the kitchen, tools, and ingredients. Most importantly, adult supervision is a must whenever a child uses the stove, oven, or sharp tools. Look for these symbols:

Your assistance, patience, and praise will pay off with tasty rewards for the family, and invaluable life skills for your child. Let the adventures in cooking beyond the basics begin!

CONTENTS

HOST A GAME DAY PARTY!

Welcome to Cool Young Chefs! If you have already used other Cool Cooking books, this series is for you. You know how to read a recipe and how to prepare ingredients. You have learned about measuring, cooking tools, and kitchen safety. Best of all, you like to cook!

This book has recipes and ideas for hosting a cool game day party. With a big game coming up you already have your theme. Make invitations and decorations in team colors. Buy or decorate tablecloths, napkins, plates, and cups with team colors too.

MAKE A GAME PLAN

A winning game day party starts with a good game plan. Choose a game and a date then make a list of people to invite. Plan your menu and make a shopping list. Shop the day before you plan to cook. Many of the recipes in this book can be made ahead of time. You can also put up decorations the day before the party.

SET IT UP

Make it easy for your guests to help themselves to food. Set all of the dishes out on a **buffet** table. Include plates, glasses, napkins, and silverware. When the work is done in advance, you can enjoy the game too!

AND YOU'RE OFF!

Have the food all set up just before your guests arrive. During the party, check the buffet table from time to time. Keep the table looking neat and the serving plates filled with food. The guests will cheer for the team, and for you!

WHAT'S THE BIG IDEA?

Besides being a good cook, a chef is prepared, **efficient**, organized, resourceful, creative, and adventurous. The Big Idea in *Cool Game Day Parties* is all about being creative.

Being a good host is as important as being a good chef. Your guests will be excited to see a table set up with great food! Remind your guests to help themselves!

Most of the recipes in this book are for food that should be served hot. Leave space on the table for the hot foods. When the food is ready to serve, put it in its place. Be sure to warn the guests if any of the dishes are hot! Most things will taste good even when they cool down, but they should start out hot. Bring the **desserts** out near the end of the game or after it's over.

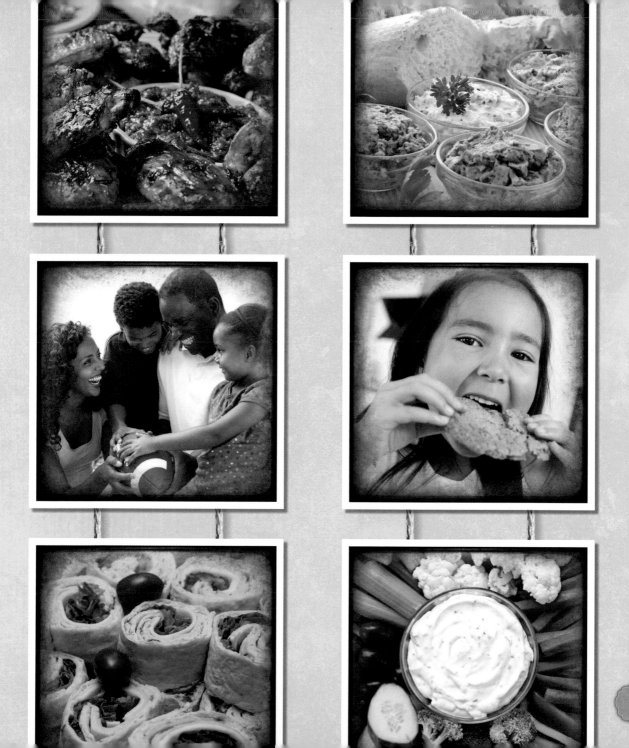

FIRST THINGS FIRST

A successful chef is smart, careful, and patient. Take time to review the basics before you start cooking. After that get creative and have some fun!

BE SMART, BE SAFE

- Start with clean hands, tools, and work surfaces.
- Always get **permission** to use the kitchen, cooking tools, and ingredients.
- Ask an adult when you need help or have questions.
- Always have an adult nearby when you use the stove, oven, or sharp tools.
- Prevent accidents by working slowly and carefully.

NO GERMS ALLOWED

After you handle raw eggs or raw meat, wash your hands with soap and water. Wash tools and work surfaces with soap and water too. Raw eggs and raw meat have bacteria that don't survive when the food is cooked. But the bacteria can survive at room or body temperature. These bacteria can make you very sick if you consume them. So, keep everything clean!

BE PREPARED

- Read through the entire recipe before you do anything else!
- Gather all the tools and ingredients you will need.
- Wash fruits and vegetables well. Pat them dry with a **towel**.
- Get the ingredients ready. The list of ingredients tells how to prepare each item.
- If you see a word you don't know, check the **glossary** on page 30.
- Do the steps in the order they are listed.

GOOD COOKING TAKES TIME

- Allow plenty of time to prepare your recipes.
- Be patient with yourself. **Prep** work can take a long time at first.

ONE LAST THING

- When you are done cooking, wash all the dishes and **utensils**.
- Clean up your work area and put away any unused ingredients.

KEY SYMBOLS

In this book, you will see some symbols beside the recipes. Here is what they mean.

The recipe requires the use of a stove or oven. You need adult **supervision** and assistance.

A sharp tool such as a peeler, knife, or **grater** is needed. Be extra careful, and get an adult to stand by.

BEYOND COOL

Remember the Big Idea? In the Beyond Cool boxes, you will find ideas to help you create your own recipes. Once you learn a recipe, you will be able to make many **versions** of it. Remember, being able to make original recipes turns cooks into chefs!

When you modify a recipe, be sure to write down what you did. If anyone asks for your recipe, you will be able to share it proudly.

GET THE PICTURE

When a step number in a recipe has a circle around it with an arrow, it will point to the picture that shows how to do the step.

③ ⟶

COOL TIP

These tips can help you do something faster, better, or more easily.

UNIQUELY COOL

Here are some of the **techniques**, ingredients, and dippers used in this book.

TECHNIQUE:

HOW TO SEPARATE AN EGG

When a recipe calls for an egg yolk, you need to separate the yolk from the egg white. Here is an easy way to do that.

Crack the egg into a small bowl. Use a **slotted** spoon to very gently lift the yolk from the bowl.

TOOLS:

CUSTARD CUPS

GLASS MEASURING CUP

SLOTTED SPOON

SLOW COOKER

STEAMER BASKET

TONGS

DIP DIPPERS:

POTATO CHIPS

TORTILLA CHIPS

CRACKERS

PITA CHIPS

SLICES OF BAGUETTE

CROSTINI

PRETZELS

CARROT STICKS

CELERY STICKS

GREEN OR RED BELL PEPPER STRIPS

BROCCOLI

CAULIFLOWER

BUFFALO CHICKEN DIP

ingredients

8-ounce package cream
  cheese, at room
  temperature

½ cup hot pepper sauce

1 cup blue cheese salad
  dressing

1 cup chopped celery

2 cups cubed cooked
  chicken

1 cup grated cheddar
  cheese

tools

measuring cups

sharp knife

cutting board

grater

large mixing bowl

hand mixer

mixing spoon

9-inch pie plate

1 Preheat the oven to 350 degrees.

2 Put the cream cheese, hot pepper sauce, and salad **dressing** in a large mixing bowl. Mix with a hand mixer.

3 Stir in the celery and cooked chicken.

4 Put the mixture in a pie plate. Bake for 30 minutes.

5 Stir in the **grated** cheese. Serve hot with chips or celery sticks, or both!

COOL TIP

Keep the dip warm for hours! Serve it in a small crockpot or fondue pot with the heat on low.

CARAMELIZED ONION DIP

MAKES 2½ CUPS

ingredients

2 tablespoons olive oil

2 large onions,
  cut in half top to bottom
  and thinly sliced

1 teaspoon sugar

1 tablespoon balsamic
  vinegar

1 cup sour cream

½ cup mayonnaise

½ teaspoon Worcestershire
  sauce

salt and pepper

tools

measuring spoons

sharp knife

cutting board

measuring cups

large saucepan

mixing spoon

mixing bowl

rubber spatula

1 Heat the olive oil in a large saucepan over medium-high heat. Add the onions. Turn the heat to low. Cook until the onions turn light brown, stirring occasionally. This can take 30 minutes or more.

2 Add the sugar and balsamic vinegar. Continue cooking over low heat until the onions are a deep caramel color. Let the onions cool.

3 Stir the onions, sour cream, and mayonnaise together in a medium mixing bowl.

4 Stir in the Worcestershire sauce and salt and pepper to taste.

COOL TIP

You can make the **caramelized** onions the day before your party. Keep them in the refrigerator in a covered bowl. Do steps 3 and 4 on the day of the party.

PERFECT PARTY PIZZA DIP

ingredients

8-ounce package cream cheese, at room temperature

1 teaspoon dried oregano

1 teaspoon dried basil

½ teaspoon garlic salt or powder

1 cup grated mozzarella cheese

½ cup grated Parmesan cheese

1 cup pizza sauce

pizza toppings, choose three of your favorites

- sliced black olives
- sliced green olives
- chopped pepperoni
- sliced mushrooms
- chopped green peppers

tools

measuring spoons

measuring cups

grater

sharp knife

cutting board

small bowl

fork

9-inch pie plate

rubber spatula

waxed paper

1. Put the cream cheese, oregano, basil, and garlic salt or powder in a small bowl. Use a fork to mash the ingredients together until well blended.

2. Spread the mixture evenly in a pie plate with a rubber spatula.

3. Sprinkle half the mozzarella cheese and half the Parmesan cheese on top.

4. Spread the pizza sauce over the cheeses. Top with your favorite pizza toppings. Sprinkle with the remaining cheese.

5. Cover the pie plate with waxed paper and microwave for 3 minutes. If the cheese isn't quite melted, microwave for another minute. Serve hot with chips or crostini (see recipe below).

BEYOND COOL

Crostini (cro-STEE-nee)

Preheat the oven to 350 degrees. Cut a baguette into ½-inch slices with a **serrated** knife. Brush olive oil on both sides of each slice. Put the slices on a baking sheet. Bake for 5 minutes. Turn the slices over and bake for 5 more minutes. Cut a clove of garlic in half. Rub one side of each bread slice with the garlic.

CLASSIC CHILI DOGS

ingredients

2 pounds ground beef

1 small onion, finely chopped (about ¾ cup)

1½ cups ketchup

¼ cup white or brown sugar

3 tablespoons white vinegar

¼ cup yellow mustard

1 teaspoon Worcestershire sauce

½ teaspoon ground black pepper

1 teaspoon salt

12 hot dogs

12 hot dog buns

pickle spears

tools

sharp knife

cutting board

measuring cups

measuring spoons

large frying pan

rubber spatula

strainer

mixing bowl

paper towels

saucepan with lid

1. Put the ground beef and onion in a large frying pan. Cook over medium-high heat. Use a rubber spatula to break up meat as it cooks. Cook the meat until it is no longer pink.

2. Put the strainer in a mixing bowl. Line it with paper **towels**. Pour in the meat and onion mixture to drain the grease.

3. Put the drained meat and onion mixture in a saucepan. Stir in the rest of the ingredients. Cover the pan. Cook over low heat for about an hour. Stir occasionally.

4. Heat the hot dogs. Put them in the buns. Let your guests top them with the chili sauce, pickle spears, and other **condiments**.

BEYOND COOL

To make it a Coney Island hot dog, top the chili sauce with yellow mustard and chopped onion. Yum!

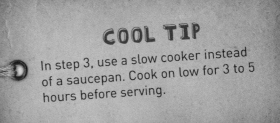

COOL TIP

In step 3, use a slow cooker instead of a saucepan. Cook on low for 3 to 5 hours before serving.

CHICAGO-STYLE HOT DOGS

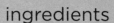

MAKES 8 CHICAGO DOGS

ingredients

8 all-beef hot dogs

8 hot dog buns

yellow mustard

½ cup sweet green pickle relish

½ cup finely chopped onion

3 tomatoes, cut into 8 wedges

8 dill pickle spears

16 sport peppers

celery salt

tools

measuring cups

sharp knife

cutting board

large saucepan with lid

tongs

steamer basket

measuring spoons

NO KETCHUP ALLOWED!

Real Chicago-style hot dogs don't need ketchup!

20

1 Bring a saucepan of water to a boil. Turn the heat to low and add the hot dogs. Heat the hot dogs for 5 minutes. Use tongs to remove the hot dogs.

2 Carefully pour out all but 1 inch of water. Put a steamer basket in the pan. Put the buns in the steamer basket and cover the pot. Steam the buns for 2 minutes or until warm. Use tongs to remove the buns.

3 Put a hot dog in each bun. Put the toppings on in this order.

- yellow mustard

- 1 tablespoon sweet green pickle relish

- 1 tablespoon chopped onion

- 2 sport peppers

- tomato wedges on one side of the hot dog

- pickle spears on the other side of the hot dog

- a sprinkle of celery salt

DELICIOUS ASIAN-STYLE WINGS

SERVES 6

ingredients

2 cloves garlic
2 tablespoons soy sauce
3 tablespoons Hoisin sauce
3 tablespoons honey
1 teaspoon sesame oil
3 pounds chicken wings
2 tablespoons sesame seeds
2 scallions, thinly sliced

tools

measuring spoons
sharp knife
cutting board
baking sheet
aluminum foil
large mixing bowl
fork
mixing spoon
paper towels
tongs
serving plate

1. Preheat the oven to 425 degrees. Cover a large baking sheet with aluminum foil.

2. Put the garlic in a large mixing bowl. Mash it with a fork. Add the soy sauce, Hoisin sauce, honey, and sesame oil. Stir until well blended.

3. Wash the chicken wings. Dry them well with paper **towels**.

4. Add the chicken wings to the bowl. Toss to coat the wings with **marinade**. Arrange the wings on the baking sheet.

5. Bake for 15 minutes. Turn the wings over. Bake for 15 more minutes. The wings should be **crispy** on the outside and no longer pink inside.

6. Put the wings on a serving plate. Sprinkle the sesame seeds and scallions over the wings.

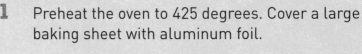
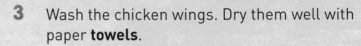

MARVELOUS MEATBALL SLIDERS

IMPORTANT!
Thick sauces such as this one can bubble and spray hot drops of sauce. Stir the sauce often to prevent eruptions.

SERVES 9

ingredients

18 small buns or rolls

SAUCE

¼ cup olive oil

1 medium onion, finely chopped

4 cloves garlic, minced

2 28-ounce cans crushed tomatoes

1 teaspoon dried basil

1 tablespoon brown sugar

salt and pepper to taste

MEATBALLS

1 cup bread crumbs

1 pound ground pork

1 pound ground beef

4 clove garlic, minced

1 cup grated Parmesan cheese

3 eggs, lightly beaten

½ cup chopped Italian flat leaf parsley

1 teaspoon dried oregano

½ teaspoon dried basil

tools

measuring cups & spoons

sharp knife

cutting board

can opener

grater

whisk

large saucepan with lid

mixing spoon

large mixing bowl

baking sheet

waxed paper

large spoon

1. Make the sauce first. Heat the oil in a large saucepan over medium-high heat. Add the onion and sauté for 5 minutes. Add the **minced** garlic and sauté for 2 more minutes, stirring constantly.

2. Add the tomatoes, basil, and brown sugar. Simmer over low heat while you make the meatballs. Stir the sauce often.

3. Put all of the meatball ingredients in a large mixing bowl. Mix with your hands until well blended.

4. Cover a baking sheet with waxed paper. Use a ¼-cup measuring cup to scoop portions of the meat mixture. Set the scoops of the meat on the baking sheet.

5. Increase the heat on the sauce to bring it to a boil. Have a helper stir the sauce to keep it from erupting.

6. Wet your hands and roll each scoop of meat into a ball. The water will help seal the meatball. Use a large spoon to set each meatball in the sauce.

7. Turn the heat to low and cook the meatballs in the sauce for at least 1 hour. Serve the meatballs and sauce on the buns.

BEYOND COOL

Use these herbs and spices to give an Italian flavor to sauces.

- basil, fresh or dried
- oregano, fresh or dried
- marjoram, fresh or dried
- Italian parsley, fresh or dried
- fennel, dried pods smashed to a powder

COOKIE ICE CREAM SANDWICHES

ingredients

SMALL ICE CREAM SANDWICHES

9-ounce box chocolate wafer cookies

1 pint ice cream, any flavor

6-ounce package mini chocolate chips

LARGE ICE CREAM SANDWICHES

2 dozen 3-inch cookies, any kind

1 quart ice cream, any flavor

12-ounce package mini chocolate chips

tools

baking sheet

ice cream scoop or spoon

plate

waxed paper

1. Put the cookies upside down on a baking sheet. Put the baking sheet in the freezer for 30 minutes.

2. Get the ice cream and the scoop ready. Prepare to work quickly!

3. Take the cookie sheet from the freezer. Put a scoop of ice cream on half of the cookies.

4. Turn over the rest of the cookies. Place one on top of each cookie with ice cream. Press down gently to spread the ice cream to the edges.

5. Put the cookie sheet back in the freezer for 1 hour.

6. Put the chocolate chips on a plate. Take one ice cream **sandwich** from the freezer at a time. Roll the side of each sandwich in the chips to coat the ice cream.

7. Freeze them for 15 more minutes. Wrap each sandwich in waxed paper. Keep them in the freezer until ready to serve.

COOL TIP

It is a little tricky to get the ice cream to just the right softness. If the ice cream is too soft or too hard, it will be hard to make good sandwiches. If the ice cream is frozen solid, let it sit out until it softens a bit. If it gets too soft, put it back in the freezer for a few minutes. Most of all, remember to work quickly!

CHOCOLATE HOT LAVA CAKES

SERVES 4

ingredients

4 ounces semi-sweet chocolate

½ cup butter

1 tablespoon milk

1 teaspoon vanilla extract

1 cup powdered sugar

2 eggs plus 1 egg yolk

6 tablespoons flour

1 teaspoon cinnamon

tools

measuring cups

measuring spoons

4 6-ounce custard cups or mini soufflé dishes

baking sheet

medium microwave-safe bowl

whisk

dinner knife

small plate

1 Preheat the oven to 425 degrees. Coat the inside of each custard cup with butter. Place them on the baking sheet.

2 Put the chocolate and ½ cup butter in a medium microwave-safe bowl. Microwave on high for 1 minute, or until butter is melted. Stir with a whisk until well blended.

3 Add the milk, vanilla, and 1 cup powdered sugar. Blend well with a whisk.

4 Add the eggs and yolk. Whisk until well blended. Add the flour and cinnamon. Whisk until the mixture is completely blended and smooth. Pour into the custard cups.

5 Bake 13 to 15 minutes or until sides and center are firm. Let them cool for 1 minute. Run a dinner knife around the edges of the cakes. Put a small plate upside down over a cake. Turn the cake and plate over together. Shake gently so the cake falls onto the plate. Repeat with the other cakes. Sprinkle the cakes with powdered sugar.

BEYOND COOL

For spiced lava cakes, replace the cinnamon with ½ teaspoon ground ginger and a **pinch** of ground cloves or allspice.

COOL TIP

You can prepare the lava cakes ahead of time. After step 4, cover the custard cups with plastic wrap and refrigerate them. Take them out of the refrigerator 30 minutes before you bake them.

GLOSSARY

buffet – a meal in which the food is set out on a table or counter for guests to serve themselves.

caramelize – to cook sugar, syrup, or honey until it turns into caramel, a sweet, brown flavoring.

condiment – something that adds flavor to food, such as a sauce or a spice.

crispy – hard, thin, and easy to break.

dessert – a sweet food, such as fruit, ice cream, or pastry, served after a meal.

dressing – a sauce that is used in salads.

efficient – able to do something without wasting time, money, or energy.

glossary – a list of the hard or unusual words found in a book.

grate – to cut something into small pieces using a grater. A grater is a tool with sharp-edged holes.

marinade – a sauce that food is soaked in before cooking.

mince – to cut or chop into very small pieces.

permission – when a person in charge says it's okay to do something.

pinch – the amount of an ingredient that can be held between your finger and thumb.

prep – short for preparation, the work done before starting to make a recipe, such as washing fruits and vegetables, measuring, cutting, peeling, and grating.

sandwich – two pieces of bread with a filling, such as meat, cheese, or peanut butter, between them.

serrated – having a sharp jagged or toothed edge, like a saw.

slotted – having narrow openings or holes.

supervision – the act of watching over or directing others.

technique – a method or style in which something is done.

towel – a cloth or paper used for cleaning or drying.

utensil – a tool used to prepare or eat food.

version – a different form or type from the original.

WEB SITES

To learn more about cool cooking, visit ABDO Publishing Company online at www.abdopublishing.com. Web sites about cool cooking are featured on our Book Links page. These links are monitored and updated to provide the most current information available.

INDEX